W9-BYE-055

MATH IN THE
ASTEROID BELT

By Mark A. Harasymiw

Gareth Stevens
PUBLISHING

Please visit our website, www.garethstevens.com. For a free color catalog of all our high-quality books, call toll free 1-800-542-2595 or fax 1-877-542-2596.

Library of Congress Cataloging-in-Publication Data

Names: Harasymiw, Mark, author.
Title: Math in the asteroid belt / Mark A. Harasymiw.
Description: New York : Gareth Stevens Publishing, [2017] | Series: Solve it!
  Math in space | Includes index.
Identifiers: LCCN 2015050135 | ISBN 9781482449372 (pbk.) | ISBN 9781482449310 (library bound) | ISBN 9781482449211 (6 pack)
Subjects: LCSH: Asteroids–Juvenile literature. | Mathematics–Juvenile
  literature.
Classification: LCC QB377 .H37 2017 | DDC 523.44–dc23
LC record available at http://lccn.loc.gov/2015050135

First Edition

Published in 2017 by
Gareth Stevens Publishing
111 East 14th Street, Suite 349
New York, NY 10003

Copyright © 2017 Gareth Stevens Publishing

Designer: Laura Bowen
Editor: Therese Shea

Photo credits: Cover, p. 1 (asteroids) Denis_A/Shutterstock.com; cover, p. 1 (metal banner) Eky Studio/Shutterstock.com; cover, pp. 1–24 (striped banner) M. Stasy/Shutterstock.com; cover, pp. 1–24 (stars) angelinast/Shutterstock.com; cover, pp. 1–24 (math pattern) Marina Sun/Shutterstock.com; pp. 4–24 (text box) Paper Street Design/Shutterstock.com; p. 5 Claus Lunau/Science Photo Library/Getty Images; pp. 7, 9, 11 (Gaspra), 13 (inset), 15 (all), 17 (albedo chart), 17 (21 Lutetia), 19 (Mathilde), 19 (Juno), courtesy of NASA.com; p. 11 (Ceres) Ron Miller/Stocktrek Images/Getty Images; p. 13 (main) PhilipTerryGraham/Wikimedia Commons; p. 19 (Kleopatra) PedroPVZ/Wikimedia Commons; p. 21 (sky) Cropbot/Wikimedia Commons; p. 21 (meteorite) Meteorite Recon/Wikimedia Commons; p. 21 (trees) Universal Images Group/Getty Images.

All rights reserved. No part of this book may be reproduced in any form without permission in writing from the publisher, except by a reviewer.

Printed in the United States of America

CPSIA compliance information: Batch #CS16GS: For further information contact Gareth Stevens, New York, New York at 1-800-542-2595.

CONTENTS

Words in the glossary appear in **bold** type the first time they are used in the text.

MISSION TO THE ASTEROID BELT

Between Mars and Jupiter is an area full of asteroids called the asteroid belt. An asteroid is a rocky object smaller than a planet that orbits, or travels around, the sun. It can be very tiny, just a few feet across, or very large—up to several hundred miles wide!

There are many different asteroids in the asteroid belt. Scientists have counted more than 670,000, but there could be millions more not yet discovered! Read on to discover more about this amazing place for yourself.

Neptune

Uranus

Mars

This image shows where the asteroid belt appears between Mars and Jupiter.

Mercury

Venus

asteroid belt

Earth

Saturn

Jupiter

YOUR MISSION

Scientists who study space and the objects in it use math. In this book, you're the space scientist. You'll complete **missions** to learn more about the asteroid belt by using math skills. Look for the upside-down answers to check your work. Good luck!

5

NOT QUITE PLANETS

Though some scientists call the objects in the asteroid belt "minor planets," they aren't considered to be planets like Earth or Jupiter. A planet is a **celestial** body nearly round in shape that's not a moon, orbits the sun, and has enough **gravity** to clear other objects from its orbital path. The asteroid belt is crowded with asteroids that share an orbital path.

YOUR MISSION

About 108,000 asteroids had been found in the asteroid belt by the end of the 20th century. Today, we know of about 670,000 asteroids there. About how many more asteroids have been found in the asteroid belt since the end of the 20th century?

$$670,000 - 108,000 = ?$$

Some asteroids have enough gravity to have their own moons! This is the asteroid Ida orbited by a moon called Dactyl.

ANSWER: About 562,000 more asteroids have been found in the asteroid belt since the end of the 20th century.

PIECES OF A PLANET

Scientists think the planets of the **solar system** formed when pieces of dust and gas **collided** and stuck together in space. Over millions of years, larger and larger bodies formed into the planets and other celestial bodies we know today, including asteroids. It's thought that the gravity of Jupiter and the sun pulled on the objects in the asteroid belt so they couldn't form planets.

YOUR MISSION

An astronomical unit (AU) is the average distance from Earth to the sun, or about 93 million miles. The asteroid belt is between 2 and 4 AUs from the sun. About how many million miles is 2 AUs? About how many million miles is 4 AUs?

93 million + 93 million = ?

93 million + 93 million + 93 million + 93 million = ?

8

Scientists believe that Mars's two moons, Phobos and Deimos, were once asteroids!

Deimos

Phobos

ANSWER: Two AUs is about 186 million miles (300 million km). Four AUs is about 372 million miles (600 million km).

HOW LARGE?

Most asteroids aren't very big. In fact, scientists guess that if all known asteroids gathered into a single round object, its **diameter** would be about 930 miles (1,500 km). Our moon's diameter is about 2,160 miles (3,475 km), more than twice that! Some asteroids are as small as a grain of sand. Others, such as the asteroid Ceres, are quite large.

YOUR MISSION

Ceres is the largest asteroid. Its diameter is about 1,570 fewer miles than the diameter of the moon, which is found above. About how many miles is the diameter of Ceres?

$$2,160 - 1,570 = ?$$

Ceres

Gaspra

The official name of an asteroid consists of a number and a word. The word is chosen by the person who discovered the asteroid. This asteroid is officially known as 951 Gaspra.

ANSWER: The diameter of Ceres is about 590 miles (950 km).

CERES: FIRST AND BIGGEST

Ceres is so large that it's considered a dwarf planet, just like Pluto is! Still, neither Ceres nor Pluto have enough gravity to clear their orbital path, so they're not planets. Ceres was the first object found in the asteroid belt. Italian **astronomer** Giuseppe Piazzi spotted it in 1801. He named Ceres after the Roman goddess of grain.

YOUR MISSION

Ceres spins around, just like Earth does. The amount of time it takes to do that once is the length of its day. A day on Ceres is about 15 hours shorter than a day on Earth. About how long is a day on Ceres?

$$24 - 15 = ?$$

Ceres (officially called 1 Ceres) has some bright spots on its surface. NASA (National Aeronautics and Space Administration) scientists think the bright spots may be huge salt **deposits**!

ANSWER: A day on Ceres is about 9 hours.

VESTA: METEORITE MAKER

The second-largest object in the asteroid belt is named Vesta (or 4 Vesta). At some point in the past, another asteroid hit Vesta and knocked about 1 percent of its **mass** into space! Scientists think that about 5 percent of the **meteorites** we find on Earth were once part of Vesta.

YOUR MISSION

Vesta is home to one of the highest mountains in the solar system! Earth's tallest mountain, Mount Everest, is about 5 1/2 miles high. Vesta's mountain is about 7 1/2 miles taller than this. About how tall is Vesta's mountain?

$$5 1/2 + 7 1/2 = ?$$

Vesta

The NASA spacecraft *Dawn* began its journey to Vesta in September 2007. It explored Vesta from 2011 to 2012.

Dawn

Vesta meteorites

ANSWER: Vesta's mountain is about 13 miles (21 km) tall.

TYPES OF ASTEROIDS

Scientists usually place asteroids into 3 main groups: C-type, S-type, or M-type. One feature of each group is albedo (al-BEE-doh), or the measure of how much light an asteroid's surface **reflects**. A white object that reflects all sunlight has an albedo of 1.0. A black object that **absorbs** all sunlight has an albedo of 0.0. C-type asteroids are dark, with an albedo of 0.03 to 0.09. S-type asteroids are brighter, with an albedo of 0.10 to 0.22. M-types have an albedo of 0.10 to 0.18.

YOUR MISSION

Study the pie chart. According to the pie chart, which type of asteroid is the most common? Are there more S-type or M-type asteroids?

THE TYPES OF ASTEROIDS

high albedo →

← low albedo

The asteroid 21 Lutetia was visited by NASA's spacecraft *Rosetta* in July 2010. It's a C-type asteroid.

21 Lutetia

M-type

other

S-type

C-type

ANSWER: The most common type of asteroid is C-type. There are more S-type asteroids than M-type asteroids.

WHAT THEY'RE MADE OF

Since spacecraft haven't visited all asteroids, scientists can only guess what they're made of. They believe most C-type asteroids are probably made of clay and **silicate** rock. Most S-type asteroids are made of silicate rock and a mixture of nickel and iron. M-type asteroids are metallic, made almost entirely of nickel and iron. Scientists sometimes find asteroids that don't fit in these groups, however.

YOUR MISSION

Asteroids Ceres, Lutetia, Siwa, and Mathilde are all C-type asteroids. Juno and Ida are S-type asteroids. What fraction of these 6 asteroids are S-type?

$$\frac{\text{S-type}}{\text{C-type} + \text{S-type}} = \frac{?}{?}$$

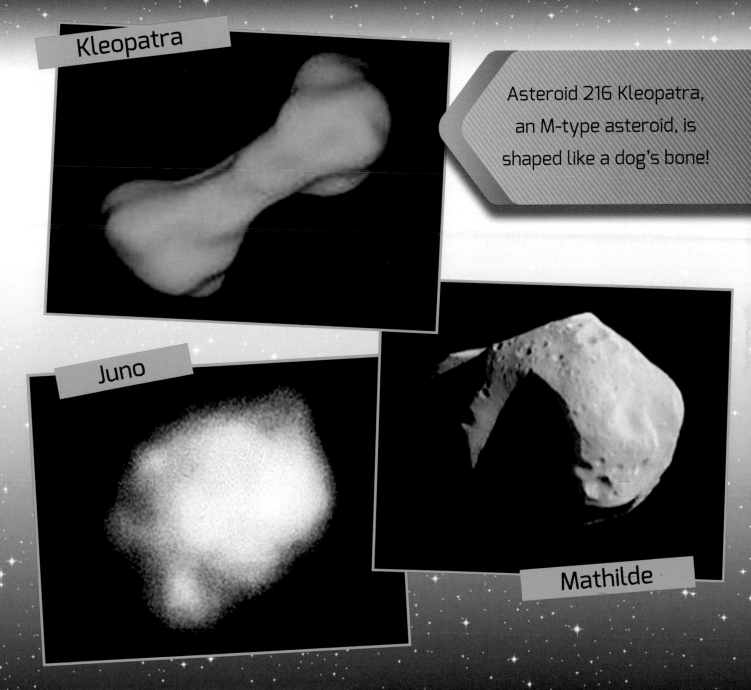

Kleopatra

Asteroid 216 Kleopatra, an M-type asteroid, is shaped like a dog's bone!

Juno

Mathilde

ANSWER: 2/6, or 1/3, of these asteroids are S-type.

DANGER TO EARTH?

Many scientists think the dinosaurs went **extinct** as a result of an asteroid hitting Earth about 65 million years ago. Asteroids get pushed or pulled out of the belt when the gravity of Jupiter, Mars, or some other celestial object pushes them out of place. Don't worry, though. Scientists are always on the watch for asteroids—in and out of the asteroid belt!

YOUR MISSION

In 2002, an asteroid passed between Earth and the moon. The moon is an average distance of about 240,000 miles from Earth. The asteroid was about 165,000 miles closer than this. About how close did the asteroid come to Earth?

$$240,000 - 165,000 = ?$$

It's thought that an asteroid about 120 feet (37 m) wide struck Siberia in Russia in 1908. These trees were flattened by the collision!

ANSWER: The asteroid came as close as about 75,000 miles (120,700 km) to Earth.

GLOSSARY

absorb: to take in

astronomer: a person who studies stars, planets, and other heavenly bodies

celestial: of or relating to the sky

collide: to hit with great force

deposit: an amount of a mineral in the ground that built up over a period of time

diameter: the distance from one side of a round object to another through its center

extinct: no longer living

gravity: the force that pulls objects toward the center of a celestial body

mass: the amount of matter in an object

meteorite: a space rock that has reached Earth's surface

mission: a task or job a group must perform

reflect: to throw back light

silicate: containing the element silicon

solar system: the sun and all the space objects that orbit it, including the planets and their moons

FOR MORE INFORMATION

Books

Dillard, Mark. *Journey Through the Asteroid Belt.* New York, NY: PowerKids Press, 2015.

Owen, Ruth. *Asteroids and the Asteroid Belt.* New York, NY: Windmill Books, 2013.

Rooney, Anne. *A Math Journey Through Space.* New York, NY: Crabtree Publishing, 2015.

Websites

Asteroids
solarsystem.nasa.gov/planets/asteroids
See pictures, photographs, and more facts about asteroids.

Dawn: First to Explore a Dwarf Planet
solarsystem.nasa.gov/missions/dawn
Learn more about the *Dawn* mission.

Publisher's note to educators and parents: Our editors have carefully reviewed these websites to ensure that they are suitable for students. Many websites change frequently, however, and we cannot guarantee that a site's future contents will continue to meet our high standards of quality and educational value. Be advised that students should be closely supervised whenever they access the Internet.

INDEX